Who Wa Claude Monet?

Who Was Claude Monet?

By Ann Waldron
Illustrated by Stephen Marchesi

Grosset & Dunlap

GROSSET & DUNLAP
Published by the Penguin Group
Penguin Group (USA) Inc., 375 Hudson Street, New York, New York 10014, USA
Penguin Group (Canada), 90 Eglinton Avenue East, Suite 700, Toronto,
Ontario M4P 2Y3, Canada (a division of Pearson Penguin Canada Inc.)
Penguin Books Ltd., 80 Strand, London WC2R 0RL, England
Penguin Group Ireland, 25 St. Stephen's Green, Dublin 2, Ireland
(a division of Penguin Books Ltd.)
Penguin Group (Australia), 250 Camberwell Road, Camberwell, Victoria 3124, Australia
(a division of Pearson Australia Group Pty. Ltd.)
Penguin Books India Pvt. Ltd., 11 Community Centre, Panchsheel Park,
New Delhi—110 017, India
Penguin Group (NZ), 67 Apollo Drive, Rosedale, North Shore 0632, New Zealand
(a division of Pearson New Zealand Ltd.)
Penguin Books (South Africa) (Pty.) Ltd., 24 Sturdee Avenue,
Rosebank, Johannesburg 2196, South Africa

Penguin Books Ltd., Registered Offices:
80 Strand, London WC2R 0RL, England

Text copyright © 2009 by Ann Waldron.
Illustrations copyright © 2009 by Stephen Marchesi.
Cover illustration copyright © 2009 by Nancy Harrison.
All rights reserved. Published by Grosset & Dunlap,
a division of Penguin Young Readers Group,
345 Hudson Street, New York, New York 10014.
GROSSET & DUNLAP is a trademark of Penguin Group (USA) Inc.
Printed in the U.S.A.

Library of Congress Control Number: 2008051458

ISBN 978-0-448-44985-2   20 19 18 17 16 15 14 13 12 11

Contents

Who Was
Claude Monet?

Claude Monet brought sunshine into painting.
He was one of the first artists to work outdoors.
That may not sound unusual to us. But before
1870, most artists did all their painting in studios.
They used models dressed up as Greek gods or

heroes from history. They painted with dark colors so their pictures would look more "serious." They might have sometimes gone outside to draw a scene, but they always came back inside to paint the finished picture.

Claude Monet and his artist friends broke the rules. Even as art students in Paris, they took their easels and paints and brushes outdoors to paint riverbanks or woods. They made trips to the seashore and painted all day long.

They wanted to show the way sunlight made water and trees and boats look at different times during the day. If they painted people, they painted ordinary people in ordinary clothes. They used bright colors and painted quickly.

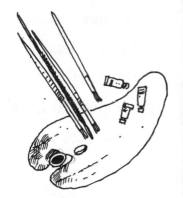

For years, Monet earned hardly any money. Sometimes he could not pay the rent; sometimes his family had no heat; sometimes they went hungry. Still, Monet would not give up.

Today, he is one of the most famous artists ever. Paintings by Monet sell for millions of dollars and hang in museums all over the world. We are all lucky that Claude never stopped believing in his art.

Chapter 1
A Boy Who Loved Drawing

The artist Claude Monet was born in Paris, France, on November 14, 1840. But when he was five, his family moved to Le Havre, a great seaport.

As a boy Claude hated school. His school was open only two hours in the morning and two hours in the afternoon. Still, he could barely stand it. School always made him feel like he was in "a prison." When the sun was shining, he wanted to be outdoors, in the fields, or by the sea. Throughout his life he was a person who never wanted to stick by the rules.

Claude's father was a grocer. He sold supplies
to the captains of the tall ships in the harbor.

Claude loved to go down to the docks. He liked to watch the men unload cargo from ships. There was mahogany from South America, sugar from the West Indies, coffee beans from Java, tea from India, and dates from Persia. He liked to hear the men speaking foreign languages.

Claude's mother died when he was sixteen. His Aunt Marie-Jeanne had no children of her own so she helped to raise him.

He was a tall, cheerful boy. He always liked to draw. He began drawing pictures of imaginary animals and funny pictures of his teachers.

AUNT MARIE-JEANNE

Claude also took drawing classes. His teacher taught the way everybody taught art then.

Students first drew pictures of statues. After years of this, the students were allowed to draw living people. If they took classes long enough, the students would learn to paint.

Claude did not like the teacher or the class. He kept on with his own drawing, using a pencil or pen and ink to turn out quick sketches of people in Le Havre. A store that sold art supplies framed

his drawings and put them in the window.
Claude sold many of his pictures.

The store owner introduced him to a local
painter. His name was Eugène Boudin. He liked

to paint landscapes—pictures of nature. Boudin invited Claude to spend the day painting with him. Claude said no at first. Boudin's little pictures sold for far less money than Claude's cartoons. Then one summer day, he gave in and bought some oil paints. Then he set out with Boudin for the country.

OIL PAINTS

WHEN MONET WAS YOUNG, LARGE PAINTINGS OF HISTORICAL SCENES OR MYTHS WERE VERY POPULAR. IT MIGHT TAKE AN ARTIST WEEKS, MONTHS, OR EVEN A YEAR TO COMPLETE A PAINTING. ARTISTS USED SHARP OUTLINES FOR EVERYTHING; NOTHING WAS SOFT OR BLURRED. THEY WORKED TOWARD AN ABSOLUTELY PERFECT FINISH. THIS REQUIRED AT LEAST THREE COATS OF PAINT.

UNTIL JUST BEFORE MONET BEGAN PAINTING, FRENCH ARTISTS WERE STILL USING THE SAME KINDS OF OIL PAINTS THAT ARTISTS HAD USED

FOR FOUR HUNDRED YEARS, THEY HAD TO GRIND
THEIR OWN PIGMENTS AND MIX THEIR OWN PAINTS.
THEY USED MANY EARTH-TONED COLORS. THERE
WAS NO WAY TO MAKE GOOD, BRIGHT, GREEN
PAINT.

BY THE MID-NINETEENTH CENTURY, NEW DYES
FOR PAINTS CAME ALONG. ARTISTS HAD NEW AND
BRIGHTER COLORS TO USE. ABOUT THE SAME

TIME, MANUFACTURERS FIGURED OUT HOW TO PUT
OIL PAINTS IN TUBES WITH SCREW TOPS. NOW
ARTISTS COULD TAKE THEIR PAINTS OUTDOORS.
JUST IN TIME FOR THE IMPRESSIONISTS!

Boudin was one of a handful of artists who painted outdoors. When Claude watched his new friend painting the sky and the fields exactly as they were, his eyes opened.

Claude's life changed.

He wanted to go to Paris to study painting. His father wanted him to go into the grocery business. But his aunt encouraged Claude. She, too, was a painter. In 1859, he left Le Havre for Paris. Claude was eighteen years old. The money from his funny pictures was more than enough to support him.

Paris was a dazzling city with cafés, nightclubs, and museums. Claude went to see the great art show known as the Salon. It was held every year in a giant glass-roofed hall. Every artist wanted his paintings to be in the Salon. Claude saw more than two thousand pictures. They hung from floor to ceiling with their frames touching. All the paintings were the type that showed famous

moments in history or myths. This type of art
didn't interest Claude at all. He thought it looked
depressing.

He enrolled in classes at the Académie Suisse,
which was free. Students contributed a little
money to pay for a model and worked on whatever they wanted to. They could draw or paint
with oils or watercolors. They could paint a live

model or they could work on a still life. They
could come any time from early in the morning
until late at night. For Claude it was like being in
heaven.

Claude worked on his drawing.
He made friends with an older
student named Camille
Pissarro. The two remained
friends all their lives.

Monet loved living in
Paris. But in 1861, this
exciting time came to
an end.

CAMILLE PISSARRO

Why?

Claude Monet had to join the French army.

Chapter 2
A Rocky Start

Monet was sent to Algeria in northern Africa. He loved the heat and the light. He thought it was romantic to sleep in a tent in the desert.

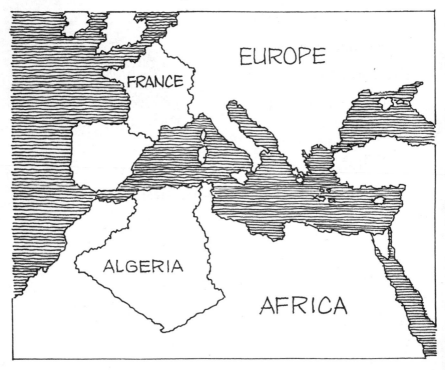

ZOUAVES

THE ZOUAVES WAS THE MILITARY UNIT THAT MONET JOINED IN 1861. THE FIRST REGIMENTS WERE MADE OF MEN FROM THE ZOUAVE REGION OF ALGERIA. LATER ON, FRENCHMEN LIKE CLAUDE MONET WERE ENLISTED AS WELL.

THE ZOUAVES HELPED FRANCE CONQUER ALGERIA AND FOUGHT FOR FRANCE IN WARS OUTSIDE AFRICA. THEY PLAYED AN IMPORTANT ROLE IN WORLD WAR I.

ZOUAVES WORE DASHING UNIFORMS WITH FULL RED OR WHITE TROUSERS TUCKED INTO SHINY BLACK BOOTS THAT CAME UP ALMOST TO THE KNEE. THEY WORE A WIDE SASH ACROSS THEIR CHEST AND A LONG COAT WITH A GOLD BRAID. A SMALL CAP TOPPED OFF THE OUTFIT.

Men were supposed to serve in the French army for seven years. But after two years, Monet caught typhoid fever and was sent home on sick leave.

That summer, in Le Havre, Monet continued to paint outdoors. He met a Dutch artist—Johan Barthold Jongkind—who, like Boudin, painted outdoors. Jongkind and Boudin were his schoolmasters, Monet said later.

JOHAN BARTHOLD JONGKIND

Monet's aunt thought that his finished paintings looked like rough sketches. But she saw how hard Claude worked. So she paid the government to let Claude out of the army for good. Then she packed him off to Paris. His father promised him an allowance if he studied with a proper art teacher. So Monet tried more art classes.

Monet's new teacher thought that he was a very good artist. However, he wanted Claude to make the models better looking than they really were. If their feet were too big, he thought Claude should make them smaller.

Monet did not agree. Not at all! He thought you should paint what you saw. Nor did he like painting inside a crowded, noisy studio. But something wonderful came out of these classes. Three of the students—Pierre-Auguste Renoir, Alfred Sisley, and Frédéric Bazille—became close friends of Claude's. For years, they all worked together. Bazille was a medical student. His parents paid for his art classes as long as he kept up with medical school. Renoir had started work as a china painter when he was only thirteen. Like Monet, he had saved enough money to come to Paris. Sisley was the lucky one, they all said. He was English. His father was a business-man in Paris and paid for his son's art studies without conditions.

MONET'S FRIENDS

MONET BECAME CLOSE FRIENDS WITH FRÉDÉRIC BAZILLE, PIERRE-AUGUSTE RENOIR, AND ALFRED SISLEY WHILE STUDYING AT CHARLES GLEYRE'S ART STUDIO IN 1862.

FRÉDÉRIC BAZILLE

BAZILLE WAS BORN IN MONTPELIER, FRANCE, IN 1841 TO A WEALTHY FAMILY. HE OFTEN PAINTED OUTDOORS WITH MONET, BUT HIS PAINTINGS WERE MORE TRADITIONAL. WHEN THE FRANCO-PRUSSIAN WAR BROKE OUT IN 1870, BAZILLE JOINED THE ZOUAVE ARMY. HE WAS KILLED IN ACTION THAT SAME YEAR.

RENOIR WAS BORN IN LIMOGES, FRANCE, IN 1841. HE WAS THE SON OF A WORKING-CLASS TAILOR. RENOIR LOVED PAINTING, AND CREATED MANY LIVELY PORTRAITS AND

SCENES OF SOCIAL LIFE. HE HAD A LONG AND SUCCESSFUL CAREER. HE DIED IN 1919.

SISLEY WAS BORN IN PARIS, FRANCE, IN 1839 TO ENGLISH PARENTS. WHILE MONET AND RENOIR OFTEN PAINTED URBAN LIFE OR SOCIAL SCENES, THE NATURAL LANDSCAPE WAS THE CENTRAL FOCUS OF SISLEY'S ARTWORK. HE DIED IN 1899.

PIERRE-AUGUSTE RENOIR

ALTHOUGH NOT AS FAMOUS AS EITHER MONET OR RENOIR, BAZILLE AND SISLEY HAVE PAINTINGS IN MANY FAMOUS MUSEUMS IN THE UNITED STATES AND EUROPE.

Monet told his new friends about painting
outdoors. At first the others weren't interested.
Renoir persuaded Monet to go with him to copy
pictures at the Louvre Museum.

But instead Monet set up his easel inside the museum and painted what he saw outside the window!

PHOTOGRAPHY

PHOTOGRAPHS WERE SHOWN IN THE PARIS SALON FOR THE FIRST TIME IN 1859. (THIS WAS A YEAR BEFORE MONET FIRST VISITED THE SALON.)

THE NEW ART OF PHOTOGRAPHY INFLUENCED YOUNG PAINTERS OF THE DAY. PHOTOGRAPHS SHOWED EVERYDAY LIFE—ORDINARY PEOPLE IN MODERN CLOTHES. THEY CAPTURED A MOMENT IN TIME. THIS IS WHAT MONET WANTED TO DO. ALSO, BECAUSE PHOTOGRAPHY PROVIDED A REALISTIC PICTURE OF ANYTHING, ARTISTS LIKE MONET AND HIS FRIENDS FELT THAT PAINTERS WERE NOW FREE TO BE LESS REAL. THEY COULD BE SUBJECTIVE AND EXPLORE THE EFFECTS OF LIGHT AND COLOR.

PHOTOGRAPHERS OFTEN WORKED OUTDOORS, CARRYING THEIR HUGE CAMERAS TO THE SAME PLACES WHERE MONET LIKED TO PAINT. OFTEN THEY SET UP THEIR EQUIPMENT BESIDE THE EASELS OF ARTISTS.

Finally Monet convinced his new friends to visit a pretty little town near a huge forest. They packed up their easels, paint boxes, canvases, and brushes and headed out. His friends made sketches outdoors and then finished their paintings later at a studio. Monet, however, did all his work outdoors. Already he was trying to capture sunshine and the way light and shadows fell on trees and grass.

In 1864, the art school closed. Monet never took another art class. He went home to Le Havre. His family was fed up. He hadn't sold a thing since the funny pictures he did as a school-boy. He should start painting the proper way!

Did Monet listen? Of course not. He went off to the seacoast and painted pictures outdoors. He sent two to the Salon in 1865 . . . and both were accepted!

He was thrilled. Newspapers praised his work. Claude sold both paintings for a nice sum of money.

Happy with this success, he began a new huge picture. The canvas was fifteen feet high and twenty feet long. Famous painters of the old school often painted their scenes from history on canvases that big. But Monet had something different in mind. He wanted to paint twelve people in everyday clothes at a picnic. He had friends come and pose for the picture. It was hard working outdoors on a canvas that big. So, unfortunately, Monet had to break his own rule and take the canvas inside to work on it. He very much hoped to enter this new picture in the Salon, but he couldn't finish it in time.

Instead, he quickly painted a life-size portrait of his beautiful new girlfriend, Camille. She had white skin and black hair. For the picture she wore a green striped dress and carried a parasol.

Again, because of time, he did the painting in his studio. *The Woman in the Green Dress* was accepted for the Salon in 1866 and was a triumph.

Were Monet's father and aunt pleased? No! They were furious. They had found out that Monet and Camille were living together but were not married.

Once again his father stopped his allowance.

Claude was twenty-five years old and Camille
was nineteen. They had no money—in fact they
owed money. They left Paris and rented a house
in a small town. Monet started on another big
picture—not as big as the picnic painting, but

still big. It was eight feet by seven feet and showed four women among trees and flowers. Camille posed for all four women. Monet swore he would paint everything outdoors. He dug a trench in the garden, so he could lower the canvas when he wanted to work on the top part.

Another painter came by one day and asked

why he wasn't working on the picture.

"The sun's not shining," Monet said.

His friend suggested that Monet could at least work on the background. But Monet explained that everything—even the background—had to be painted in sunlight. That was the whole point of his art.

The Salon of 1867 turned down his big new picture, *Women in the Garden*. It was too different. The sunlight shining on the dresses and parasols and the shadows from the tree looked strange to the judges.

Monet was almost out of his mind with despair. Nevertheless he kept on painting. He had no money to buy canvases. Sometimes he scraped the paint off old paintings he'd done so he could paint new pictures.

Bazille felt sorry for Monet and bought *Women in the Garden*. He promised to send some of the money every month. But lots of times he forgot. Monet was desperate. Camille was going to have a baby. Sometimes there wasn't enough money for food.

Monet was in a jam. He took Camille to Paris where he sold two pictures. He gave the money to Camille so that she had something to live on.

Then Monet went back alone to Le Havre. He decided to pretend to his parents that he and Camille had broken up.

Back in Le Havre he worked like crazy. Every bit of money he earned would go to Camille. He painted twenty pictures—people, landscapes, seascapes. More than anything, he hoped to

afford to be with Camille when the baby came.
But on August 8, 1867, little Jean was born
without his father there.

Finally Monet's aunt took pity on him and gave him money for train fare to Paris. He and Camille and the baby lived in a small rented room. It was freezing cold that winter, and the family sometimes went without heat or enough food.

Bad luck seemed to follow Monet everywhere. He sold no paintings. He and Camille and the

baby moved to a cheaper place in the country. But when he couldn't pay the rent there either, the landlady threw them out. She kept his clothes, canvases, paints, and brushes.

Now, except for his family, Monet had nothing.

Chapter 3
Bad Times and Good Times

It is hard to imagine things getting any worse for Monet. And fortunately, at last, his luck changed . . . at least a little bit. A rich man in Le Havre wanted paintings—paintings by Monet. He wanted some portraits. So Monet did them as fast as he could. The man also bought two paintings of the sea.

With this money, Monet rented a cottage for his family in a little town on the coast near Le Havre. He kept on working outside, experimenting with light and shadows. He studied the light, so he could make the light in his paintings look real. He began to use different colors of paint instead of black to paint shadows. He stopped mixing colors on his palette. Instead he painted pure colors right on the canvas. If he wanted green, Monet put a tiny brush stroke of pure blue paint next to a dot of pure yellow. When he looked at the picture, his eyes blended the blue and the yellow and saw green. He once said, "When you go out to paint, try to forget what objects you have before you, a tree, a house, a field, or whatever. Merely think, here is a little square of blue, here an oblong of pink, here a streak of yellow, and paint it just as it looks to you, the exact color and shape."

That summer, Monet spent a lot of time with his old friend, Pierre-Auguste Renoir. The two painters worked outdoors together, side by side. Monet was still poor. Renoir was poor, too. But he was living with his parents. Sometimes he would bring over bread for Monet's family to keep them from starving.

The two friends may have been poor and hungry, but they loved the work they were doing.

They both painted pictures of a happy, busy
outdoor restaurant on the Seine River. The sun
shined on the people and boats and made lovely

shadows on the water. Both their paintings of
the restaurant would later become famous.

Yet in 1870, once again the Salon rejected

Monet's pictures. His best friends—Bazille, Renoir, Sisley, and Pissarro—all had paintings accepted that year.

It was a hard time. But one good thing happened that year. Camille's parents said they would forgive her and even help support little Jean if she and Monet were married. So that's what Claude and Camille did. The wedding was in Paris. None of Monet's family came.

The bride and groom and little Jean went to
a beach resort near Le Havre. Boudin and his
wife joined them there. Monet painted pictures
of Camille on the beach. Over the years, he was
to paint her many, many times—on hillsides, in

poppy fields, with a parasol, in a garden—often
with little Jean at her side.

In July, France went to war with the country
of Prussia. (Prussia became part of what today
is modern Germany.) Monet had a family to
support; he fled to England to avoid the army.

JAPANESE PRINTS

ONE DAY MONET BOUGHT SOME GROCERIES THAT WERE WRAPPED IN PAPER THAT TURNED OUT TO BE JAPANESE PRINTS.

MONET WAS FASCINATED WITH THESE WOODCUT PRINTS, AS WERE MANY OTHER IMPRESSIONIST PAINTERS. THEY ADMIRED THE BRIGHT COLORS, FLAT, TWO-DIMENSIONAL STYLE, AND COMPOSITIONS THAT WERE OFTEN OFF-CENTER.

OVER THE YEARS MONET COLLECTED MANY PRINTS BY NOTED JAPANESE ARTISTS. THEY STILL HANG IN HIS HOUSE AT GIVERNY. JAPANESE PRINTS GAVE HIM THE IDEA FOR THE JAPANESE BRIDGE HE BUILT OVER THE POND THERE.

In London, he painted just as furiously as he had in France. And he had another stroke of luck. An older French painter introduced him to an important art dealer. His name was Paul Durand-Ruel. Durand-Ruel had a gallery in London as well as in Paris. Durand-Ruel saw Monet's talent. He bought several paintings and paid him well.

PAUL DURAND-RUEL

After the war ended, Monet didn't return to France right away. He took his family to Holland. They settled near Amsterdam where Monet painted canals and windmills and tulips.

In 1871, they went back to France and rented a house in a little town on the Seine River. Monet always liked to be near water. More than anything, he loved to paint water. He turned out nearly fifty pictures the first year.

Finally, Monet was making some real money. His family had enough to eat. Monet bought a barge, which he turned into a floating studio so he could paint in the middle of the river.

France was at peace and times were good. Durand-Ruel came back to Paris and bought more pictures from Monet. Monet painted pictures of the river, the fields, and Camille and Jean outdoors. It was a happy time.

Chapter 4
A New "Salon"

Year after year, Monet's paintings were still being rejected by the Salon. More often than not, his three friends—Renoir, Pissarro, and Sisley—were also turned down. They all thought their pictures looked fresh and lively, even if critics said they looked "sketchy" and "unfinished."

Monet thought that if they were ever going to make any money, they had to put on their own show.

So in 1874, that's what they did.

It started two weeks before the Salon show opened. Thirty artists took part.

Each day only about one hundred people came to look at their pictures, while thousands flocked to the Salon.

Visitors to the show made fun of it. Not many
pictures were sold. People were puzzled by the
dabs of bright paint on a canvas. They said each
artist must have loaded a gun with paint and
fired away at a canvas. They made the most jokes
about Monet's paintings. A critic wrote that
"Monsieur Monet . . . seems to have declared war
on beauty."

Claude Monet. 72

One of Monet's paintings was of two little boats with a red sun rising. The picture needed a title for the exhibit catalog. Monet decided to call it *Impression: Sunrise*. What made him choose this name? Monet and his friends often talked about the importance of catching the first impression of a scene in a painting.

People made fun of the title. Soon all the painters in the show were being called "Impressionists." It was meant as an insult. But

Monet and the other painters cheerfully agreed that they were indeed Impressionists.

The Impressionists continued to hold their own show for several years. At the one in 1875, police had to keep people from destroying the canvases with canes and umbrellas. Only a few pictures were sold, and those brought very low prices.

Monet once again was asking his friends for loans. Things looked really dark in the fall of 1876, when Camille became ill.

Once again, a rich art collector came to Monet's rescue. This time a man named Ernest and his wife Alice bought lots of Impressionist

ALICE AND ERNEST

paintings. They were part owners of a Paris
department store and they had a large, beautiful
home not far from Paris. Ernest asked Monet to
come stay there and paint some panels in one of
the rooms.

In 1876, Monet spent all summer working at
Ernest's house. Camille and Jean joined him there

for part of the time. They had good food, servants, and pleasant company. It must have been a wonderful rest for Camille, who was thin and sick.

Once back in Paris, Monet became interested in painting train stations. He painted the crowds, the steam coming from the huge, black locomotives, and the sky through the glass roof of the station. One stationmaster liked to help out Monet. He would order the engineers to blow white smoke if that was what Monet wanted for a picture.

However, at the next Impressionists' show, visitors hated the train station pictures, too. One man demanded the money for his ticket back. Monet earned very little money from his paintings. He had to give sixteen pictures to an art supplies dealer in order to pay the bill for his paints. Worst of all, Camille was growing sicker. She was also expecting another baby.

Chapter 5
Hardest Times

The Monets' second child, a little boy named Michel, was born in the spring of 1878. Camille's health was worse than ever. Ernest lost all his money so he and his wife Alice and their six children moved in with the Monets. Everyone

lived in a big house that had steep steps leading down to the Seine.

Alice did the housekeeping and looked after Camille and the baby Michel. She also gave piano lessons to earn money. Ernest never paid his share of household expenses and ran up bills.

It was a long, hard winter. The cold weather broke records. It started snowing on November 29 and kept on snowing all through December. The snow was several feet deep. Trains often didn't run. Often the roads were blocked. When the Seine froze, the children had fun walking across the river to the town on the other side. The grown-ups, however, were worried and miserable. Monet continued to paint outdoors. Sometimes he would wear three coats and use a hot water bottle to stay as warm as possible.

A neighbor came to their rescue. He bought some of Monet's pictures, which kept everyone from starving.

Monet sent twenty-nine pictures to the Impressionist salon that year. Mary Cassatt, an American painter in Paris, bought one of them for three hundred dollars. But many people still thought his style was odd looking. One art reviewer said he must have done all twenty-nine paintings in one afternoon.

Besides all the money troubles, Camille was dying of cancer. Monet was frantic to find a way to pay for the doctor and Camille's medicine. He pawned everything to raise as much cash as he could.

And for the first time, he could not paint.

Camille, in great pain, died on September 5, 1879.

Strange as it sounds, Monet decided to paint one last picture of her on her deathbed. He was shocked to discover that even in grief, he noticed the way the light shone on the still face of his beloved wife. In the picture, she does not look

like an angel at peace. She looks like a dead woman. He was a slave to his art, he admitted to a friend. Nothing mattered more to him.

Alice and her children remained in the house with Monet and his two boys. The next winter was as cold as the one before. The Seine froze solid again. All eight children were sick.

Monet was painting again and worked on many pictures of the Seine that winter. He never grew tired of studying the effect of light on ice and snow. After the thaw came, chunks of ice

floated down the river. Monet painted them, too, using gloomy grays and dark purples. When these pictures were put up for sale, everyone said they looked even more unfinished than his usual work.

In a town on the coast near Le Havre, he painted seascapes. One day a heavy rain began to fall. A storm was brewing. Monet decided to try

and paint it. He set up his easel on a cliff over-
looking the sea and latched it down with rope.
He kept painting while waves broke against the
cliff just below him. The waves got higher. Monet
painted away.

Then a giant wave came in and knocked him off his perch into the water. Monet was almost swept out to sea. He survived by holding on to the rope tied to his easel. Then at last, two fishermen in a boat rescued him.

Soon after this adventure, Monet moved everyone closer to Paris where there was a good school for little Jean. Alice and her six children were now a permanent part of the family. Alice felt that the two Monet boys needed her.

The family did not stay long in the new house. Monet said he couldn't paint there because the light was all wrong. Nevertheless, he made more money that year, 1882, than he ever had. The end for Monet was when the Seine overflowed and flooded the first floor. It was time to find a proper place with wonderful light where he could settle down and paint.

He searched up and down villages along the Seine River. At last he came upon a house that was nearly perfect for him. It was in a town called Giverny. He stayed there for forty-three years, the rest of his life.

Chapter 6
Giverny

Monet first saw Giverny in April. Apple trees were in bloom and wild flowers sparkled in the fields.

Monet was on a train, but he got off. Right beside the main road was a big farmhouse for rent. It was beautiful. The walls were pink; it had a slate roof and gray shutters. At each end of the house was a low barn with a dirt floor.

The house came with two acres of land that included an apple orchard and a walled garden. A path led down to the railway and, on the other side of the tracks, was a small river.

It was an ideal spot for a painter. Monet could see willow trees and all sorts of plants along the river, and lines of tall poplars marking the edges

of meadows. "I can produce masterpieces here,"
Monet said.

He first rented the house. (Later on he bought
it.) The family came with all their furniture and
Monet's boats. He now had four—the studio
boat, two rowboats, and a skiff. He moored the

boats at a place called Nettle Island. It was an easy walk from the house to Nettle Island.

Monet turned one of the dirt-floored barns into a studio. Later, he built a second studio that was much larger and had a skylight. He planted a vegetable garden. It was the job of the children to weed and water it. He tore out the hedges around the gardens. They looked too neat and orderly. He also began work on a big flower garden. (Irises

were his favorite flower.) He planted climbing
roses on metal arches over the walkways and
filled the flower beds with all sorts of plants and
flowers. He wanted to make sure there was something blooming from early spring until late fall.

Next to painting, the garden at Giverny
became the most important thing in his life. It,
too, was a work of art.

Monet was a man of habit. He got up every

day at sunrise, ate some bread and sausage, and set out with his palette and paints and easel in a wheelbarrow. He wore a beret and wooden shoes like the local farmers wore. He came back home for lunch. It was always served at 11:30 A.M. on the dot. After the meal, he would drink a cup of coffee in his studio and sometimes a glass of brandy as well. Then he went back to paint outside if the light was still good.

When he was pleased with his work, the
whole family was happy. If a picture didn't turn
out the way he wanted it to, he got rid of it.
Monet had a terrible temper. Once he was
painting on his studio boat and got so mad at the
way the picture looked that he threw the canvas
in the river and his paints and brushes after it.
He swore that he would never paint again.

The next day, of course, he had changed his mind. The trouble was that it was Sunday. No art supply store was open. Monet sent a telegram to a paint dealer in Paris. The man opened his store and sent everything Monet needed on the next train to Giverny.

Many things could upset Monet. If a meal was bad or a tree branch fell in the garden, it could send him into a rage.

In spite of bad moments like this, life was so much better than it had ever been. Monet paid more attention to the children—Alice's children, as well as his own sons, Jean and Michel. During school vacations, all eight children and Alice went with Monet to the countryside. While he painted, the children found plenty of ways to enjoy themselves. Blanche painted. Michel fished. Suzanne read. Alice sewed. The younger boys liked to catch frogs. In the summer, they all went swimming from the studio boat, taking turns

diving off the roof of the cabin into the water.
In the winter, they went ice-skating on the
frozen river.

Monet was in his forties, tall and handsome, with a huge beard. Alice was good-looking, smart, and friendly. She understood Monet and admired his work. In 1892, Alice and Monet were married. And life continued happily.

By this time, public opinion was changing. People were beginning to admire Impressionist paintings. Monet made more money. There was now a cook and an assistant cook at Giverny.

One of his favorite dishes was red beans cooked in wine. He also liked goose liver and fancy mushrooms called truffles.

Lots of guests came to visit. Besides having such a large family, Monet kept up with many friends, painters, and writers. He and Alice also liked to spend time in Paris seeing friends. They enjoyed going to a concert, the opera, or a wrestling match.

As for his art, Monet began painting series of pictures. Each series would be of the same object or of the same scene shown in different light.

One of the first of these series were paintings of rows of poplar trees along the river. Monet painted a picture of the poplars early in the morning, then one around noon, and another in late evening. He painted the trees on a cloudy day, in bright sunshine. He painted them in all seasons—in spring, summer, fall, and winter.

One day he heard that some of his favorite

poplars were going to be cut down and sold for lumber. Monet paid to have the trees remain for a few months longer so he could finish painting them.

Monet also painted haystacks in the fields. These haystacks were fifteen to twenty feet tall. Just as he had with the poplars, he painted the

haystacks again and again in different light at
different times of the year. He would arrive in
the fields with a wheelbarrow full of canvases.
Sometimes one of Alice's daughters would also
come along, bringing a second wheelbarrow with
more canvases.

Monet would start painting on one canvas. As
the day wore on and the light changed, he would
put it aside and start another. The next day, he

would go back to the first canvas and do more work on it. He'd paint each canvas at the same time every day. It was so important to him that the light remained constant.

Monet worked on another famous series of paintings of a cathedral in the city of Rouen. For these pictures, he rented a small room across from the cathedral and set up his easel by the window. Again, he tried to paint different effects,

working when the weather was misty, when there was bright sunshine, and at different times of the day in different seasons. This series of paintings was immensely popular and the cathedral paintings sold for large sums of money. They were shown in exhibits around the world.

Claude Monet was famous now.

His garden was famous, too. Strangers came to Giverny to look at the amazing flowers in the garden. Painters from all over the world came to Giverny, hoping to learn from Monet. (He told them: "Look at nature.") At one time, over forty American painters were renting rooms near Monet's house in Giverny.

The lady who ran a café in town learned to cook things that the American visitors liked, such as baked beans. She even served them a Thanksgiving dinner. Some of the Americans liked Giverny so much that they ended up buying houses there.

Alice and Claude's children were becoming
adults. Jean Monet trained as a chemist in
Switzerland. Then he went to work for his uncle
in Rouen. Jean fell in love and later married
Alice's daughter Blanche. Jean and Blanche lived

in Rouen. But they came back to Giverny every
weekend.

Michel Monet and Alice's son Jean-Pierre were
almost the same age. They were stepbrothers, but
they also became very close friends. They were

both interested in flowers and plants. Jean-Pierre even wrote a book with a family friend about the plants in the area.

Michel and Jean-Pierre were also crazy about bicycles and engines. Jean-Pierre devised a bicycle for two that had a motor. Michel built a gas-powered vehicle that looked like an early automobile.

Michel never had a job. He liked living on the farm at Giverny. And Monet liked having Michel around. The story is that the father and son never talked much. They simply greeted each other in the morning by saying "Bonjour, Monet," and "Au revoir, Monet" when they went to bed.

Chapter 7
The Garden and the Water Lilies

Monet spent more and more time and money on his garden. He enriched the chalky soil. He bought rare plants. He built more trellises for roses. He bought more land for a vegetable garden so he could use all the beds in his garden for flowers. At one point he had six gardeners working for him. But Monet was always in charge.

With so much money coming in, Monet was
able to buy some land across from his house.
There, the river formed a small pond where
arrowheads and water lilies grew. Monet added
more water lilies, all different kinds. A few years
later he bought more land so he could enlarge his
pond. He had to have ditches dug to bring water
from the river to fill his pond. It ended up being
three times bigger than the original pond.

In 1892, he began to paint pictures of water lilies. This was his last and probably most famous series. He painted the lilies and their reflections in the water.

Sadly, Alice was now suffering from a blood disease called leukemia. Her doctors could do nothing to save her. She died in 1911.

Monet was desolate without her. He was seventy years old. Often he was dizzy and weak. Worst of all, his eyesight was failing. He had cataracts, which are like thick layers of film that cover the irises. They changed how he saw colors.

Then his son Jean Monet died. Jean was only forty-seven years old. His wife Blanche came back to Giverny and helped to take care of her step-father.

Because of grief and fear for his eyes, Monet did not paint for a while.

When Monet finally picked up a brush again, he began to paint more water lilies. Now he no longer started work as soon as it was light, but

waited until his water lilies opened around noon. In 1909, forty-eight water lily pictures were in a show in Paris. People loved the paintings and said they were not like any other pictures in the world.

He began working on huge murals of the water lilies. These paintings were far bigger than any Monet had ever done before. He wanted to see these murals placed permanently in a huge circular room.

GEORGES CLEMENCEAU

In 1918, at the end of World War I, Georges Clemenceau, the prime minister of France came to Giverny. He was a friend of Monet's and asked the artist to give the water lily paintings to France. Monet agreed to donate twelve big panels if they would be displayed in a round room

where visitors could stand in the middle and be surrounded by water lilies.

The French government would not build a special building. However, there was an empty building near the Louvre Museum. It was called the Orangerie because it was where orange trees were once grown for the royal family of France. The water lily panels could hang in two oval-shaped rooms on the first floor. The government agreed that nothing else would be exhibited there.

Monet said painting was now the only thing left in his life that gave him any pleasure. Yet because Monet's eyesight was now much worse, he often wasn't satisfied with the work he did. And if he didn't like a painting, he always wanted to get rid of it. He'd cut up canvases, although sometimes Michel and Blanche would save the pieces.

Finally, when he was nearly blind, his family convinced Monet to have surgery on his eye. After two operations and new glasses, he could see well enough to paint. However, afterward he often complained about the way he saw colors.

By 1918 he had finished thirty large canvases, but he refused to sell any of them. He was nearly eighty. Yet every day he set out for the water lily pond. Two gardeners carried his easel and canvases down the path and set everything up for him.

He was very ill now. Monet had been a chain-smoker all his life and he had developed lung cancer. However, right up until the day he died on December 5, 1926, Monet worked on the water lilies. And until the very end, he was still planning new things for his garden. He was excited because some new Japanese water lily bulbs had arrived and he was eager to plant them.

Today people flock to museums to see Monet's paintings. His large water lily paintings still hang in

the Orangerie. The smaller water lily paintings hang in museums all over the world.

Michel Monet was eighty-eight years old when he died. He had no children so he left many beautiful paintings by his father to a museum in Paris. Among them is the one of the boat at sunrise that gave Impressionism its name.

The paintings by the man who often could not keep food on the table now bring prices that would have astonished Monet. One of the water lily paintings he did in 1904 sold in 2007 for $36.7 million. Monet wanted his work to sell. But money was never the most important thing to him.

When his water lily murals first went on view in the Orangerie museum, a reviewer marveled at the magical portraits of flowers in water and Monet's amazing talent to catch "fleeting moments."

This truly sums up what Monet had been doing all his life—painting fleeting moments in nature.

GIVERNY TODAY

AFTER CLAUDE MONET DIED, HIS SON MICHEL INHERITED THE HOUSE. HE DID NOT LIVE THERE, HOWEVER. BLANCHE, JEAN'S WIFE, LOOKED AFTER THE HOUSE AND GARDENS UNTIL SHE DIED IN 1947.

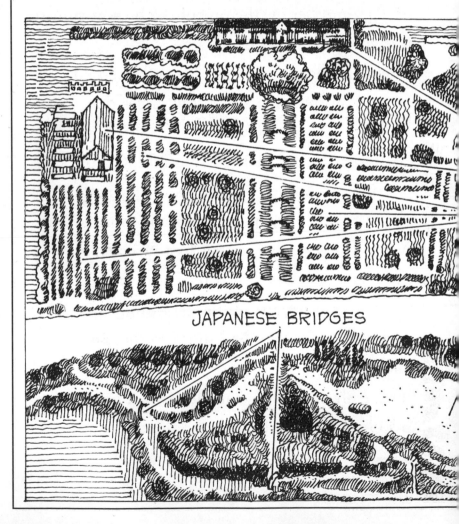

JAPANESE BRIDGES

MAIN HOUSE

GREENHOUSE

FORMAL FLOWER
GARDENS

WATER LILY
POND

AFTER MICHEL'S DEATH
IN 1966, SEVERAL AMERICAN
FOUNDATIONS HELPED RAISE
MONEY TO BRING THE HOUSE
AND ITS GARDENS BACK TO
GLORY. IT IS NOW OPEN TO THE
PUBLIC FROM APRIL THROUGH
OCTOBER. THOUSANDS OF
VISITORS COME EACH YEAR.

TIMELINE OF CLAUDE MONET'S LIFE

1840 — Claude Monet is born

1858 — Monet meets the painter Eugene Boudin

1859 — Monet moves to Paris and enters the Académie Suisse

1861 — Monet joins the Zouaves

1862 — Monet meets Bazille, Renoir, and Sisley

1865 — Monet meets Camille Doncieux

1867 — Son Jean is born

1874 — Monet exhibits *Impression: Sunrise* at the first Impressionist exhibition

1878 — Son Michel is born

1879 — Camille dies

1883 — Monet moves into the house at Giverny

1892 — Monet marries Alice Hoschedé; Monet begins to paint pictures of the water lilies

1911 — Alice dies

1914 — Jean dies

1926 — Monet dies

1927 — Orangerie Museum displays the *Water Lilies* series

TIMELINE OF THE WORLD

The world's first adhesive postage stamp, the Penny — **1840**
Black, is used

The California Gold Rush begins — **1848**

Vincent van Gogh is born — **1853**

Florence Nightingale founds the first professional — **1860**
school for nurses in England

The Thirteenth Amendment to the United States — **1865**
Constitution ends slavery in the United States

The Franco-Prussian war begins — **1870**

The Adventures of Tom Sawyer by Mark Twain — **1876**
is published;
Alexander Graham Bell invents the telephone

The Statue of Liberty is dedicated in New York Harbor — **1886**

The first Kodak box camera is sold — **1888**

The Eiffel Tower is built in Paris, France — **1889**

Marie Curie discovers radium — **1898**

Walt Disney is born — **1901**

The *New York World* newspaper publishes crossword — **1913**
puzzles for the first time

World War I begins — **1914**

The *Jazz Singer* debuts as the first talking film — **1927**

BIBLIOGRAPHY

Barrier Bjork, Christine. **Linnea in Monet's Garden.** Farrar, Straus, and Giroux, New York, 1987.

Muhlberger, Richard. **What Makes A Monet A Monet?** Viking Juvenile, New York, 2002.

Packard, Steven. **Smart About Art: Claude Monet: Sunshine and Waterlilies.** Grosset & Dunlap, New York, 2001.

Venezia, Mike. **Monet.** Children's Press, Chicago, 1990.

Waldron, Ann. **First Impressions: Claude Monet.** Harry N. Abrams, New York, 1991.

Welton, Jude. **Eyewitness Books: Monet.** DK Publishing, Inc., New York, 1999.

Where to Find Monet Paintings

Now that you know all about Claude Monet's life, you should see his paintings. Many museums in the United States have at least one painting by Monet. Here is a list of larger museums that have many Monet paintings in their permanent collections:

The Museum of Fine Arts – Boston, MA
Art Institute of Chicago – Chicago, IL
The Getty – Los Angeles, CA
Metropolitan Museum of Art – New York, NY
Philadelphia Museum of Art – Philadelphia, PA
National Gallery of Art – Washington, DC

Try to visit one if you can!